To Kathyrn and Richard

ACKNOWLEDGMENT

Both the author and illustrator wish to thank Douglas A. Lawson, Ph.D., of the Paleoecological Research Institute and Museum, Bartlesville, Oklahoma, for his expert checking of the text and illustrations. His advice was invaluable.

Lothrop, Lee & Shepard Books
New York

Pterosaurs,

Library of Congress Cataloging in Publication Data   Sattler, Helen Roney.   Pterosaurs, the flying reptiles.   Summary: Introduces the various species of flying reptiles, probably covered with fur or long hair, possibly warm-blooded, and known only from fossil evidence, which inhabited the earth in the age of dinosaurs.   1. Pterosauria—Juvenile literature.   [1. Pterodactyls.   2. Prehistoric animals. 3. Fossils]   I. Santoro, Christopher, ill. II. Title.   QE862.P7S28 1985   567.9′7   84-4428   ISBN 0-688-03995-2   ISBN 0-688-03996-0 (lib. bdg.)

the Flying Reptiles

HELEN RONEY SATTLER

Illustrations by Christopher Santoro

Sparrow-size Anurognathus

Millions of years ago, when dinosaurs roamed the earth, pterosaurs flew in the skies. Some people think that pterosaurs were dinosaurs, but they were not. They were no more closely related to dinosaurs than they were to crocodiles.

However, like dinosaurs, they are called archosaurs, or "ruling reptiles." They are classed as reptiles because they had reptilian skulls and teeth. But these remarkable animals were very special reptiles. So special that some think they should not be called reptiles at all. Reptiles of today are cold-blooded and have scaly bodies. Some pterosaurs had fur or long hair, and they may have been warm-blooded. Also, pterosaurs could fly.

Diplodocus

The first pterosaur fossils were found more than two hundred years ago. In 1831, a German scientist saw what he thought were furlike impressions in the fine-grained stone that surrounded the bones of a pterosaur. He suspected that pterosaurs were covered with fur.

A few paleontologists agreed with him. Only a warm-blooded animal could have enough energy to fly, they reasoned. And if pterosaurs were warm-blooded, they must have had fur or feathers to keep themselves warm. However, most paleontologists did not agree. They insisted that pterosaurs were reptiles, and reptiles do not have fur.

Then in 1970, a scientist found fossils of a pigeon-size pterosaur in the Soviet Union. This pterosaur was certainly covered with fur. Very clear impressions of long, thick hair could be seen in the fine-grained stone that surrounded the bones. The entire body, except for the long tail, was covered with the hair. Some of it was more than two inches long. The scientist named this new pterosaur *Sordes pilosus*, which means "hairy or shaggy devil."

Sordes pilosus

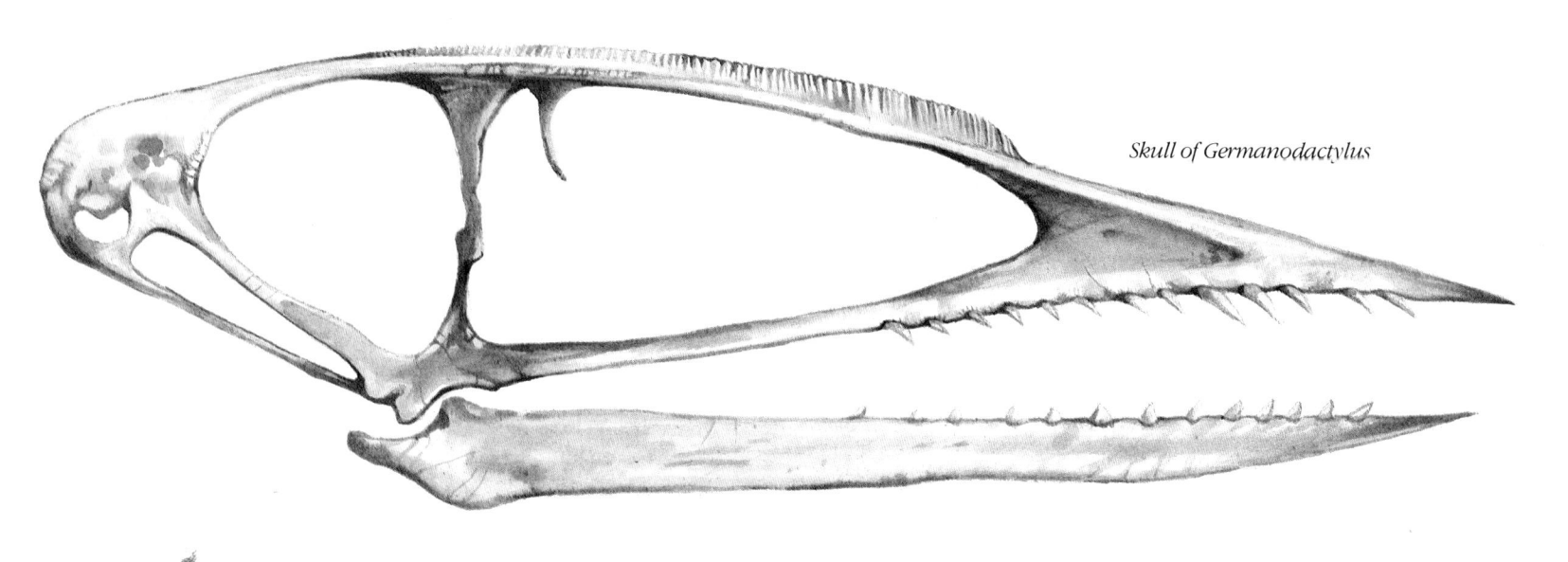

Pteranodon

Pterosaurs had wings that were similar to those of bats. A long, leathery flap of skin stretched from the tip of the enormously long fourth finger along the side of the body down to the knee. Other flaps of skin stretched from the wrist to the neck, and, in some, between the legs. The finger supporting the front edge of the wing was longer than the rest of the entire arm. The other three fingers of each hand were short and ended in long sharp claws.

Pterosaurs were light-weight. They had hollow bones filled with air pockets like those of birds. And, although they had very large heads, the skull bones were lightened with large holes.

Skull of Germanodactylus

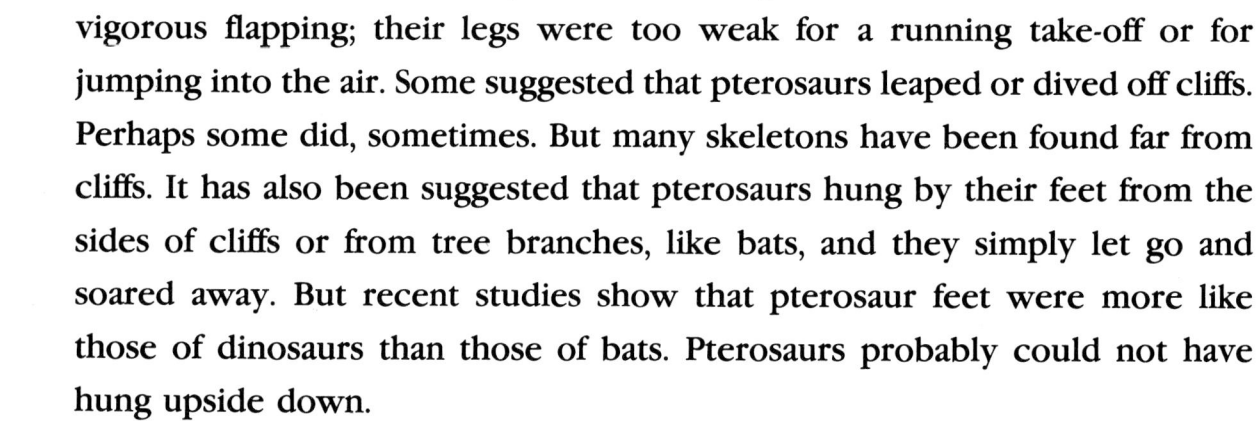

Dimorphodon

For a long time, scientists could not understand how large pterosaurs got off the ground. The thin wing bones of these pterosaurs seemed too weak for vigorous flapping; their legs were too weak for a running take-off or for jumping into the air. Some suggested that pterosaurs leaped or dived off cliffs. Perhaps some did, sometimes. But many skeletons have been found far from cliffs. It has also been suggested that pterosaurs hung by their feet from the sides of cliffs or from tree branches, like bats, and they simply let go and soared away. But recent studies show that pterosaur feet were more like those of dinosaurs than those of bats. Pterosaurs probably could not have hung upside down.

Scientists now think that a large pterosaur needed only to stand on its hind legs, face into the wind, and spread its long, strong wings. A light breeze would carry it aloft like a kite or a scrap of paper. Albatross and gooney birds of today use this method. On a still day, at least some pterosaurs could have flapped their wings fast enough for lift-off. Studies show that it would have taken only one flap per second.

Pteranodons

Most pterosaurs may have spent the greater part of their lives on the wing.
Once in the air pterosaurs, like pelicans, may have been graceful creatures.
Some soared on air currents, swooping low over the warm inland seas, lakes,
or streams to snatch surfacing fish. Others gently flapped over tropical jungles
as they searched for insects.

On the ground, it was a different story. Many probably waddled awkwardly
on their weak feet, like penguins. It was once thought that pterosaurs walked
on all fours, using their wing claws for support. Most scientists now think that
they walked on two legs, like birds.

All pterosaurs were meat-eaters. Most ate fish or insects and were probably good hunters. They had quite large, birdlike brains and must have been fairly intelligent animals. They hunted by sight. Their eyes were huge. But they had a poor sense of smell.

Most scientists think that pterosaurs laid eggs. Pterosaur fossils have been found near many pine needles that may be the remains of nests. They may have nested on barren islands, where they would have been safe from meat-eating dinosaurs like *Ornitholestes* or *Microvenator.*

Nesting Pteranodons

Young pterosaurs were probably very small and immature. They would have needed a lot of attention from their parents for food, warmth, and, later on, for flying lessons. Perhaps males brought food to their mates and young. Many had pelican-like pouches under their horny beaks.

Pterosaurs may have lived in rookeries, like penguins, or in colonies, like bats. Thousands of fossil fragments of small pterosaurs have been found together.

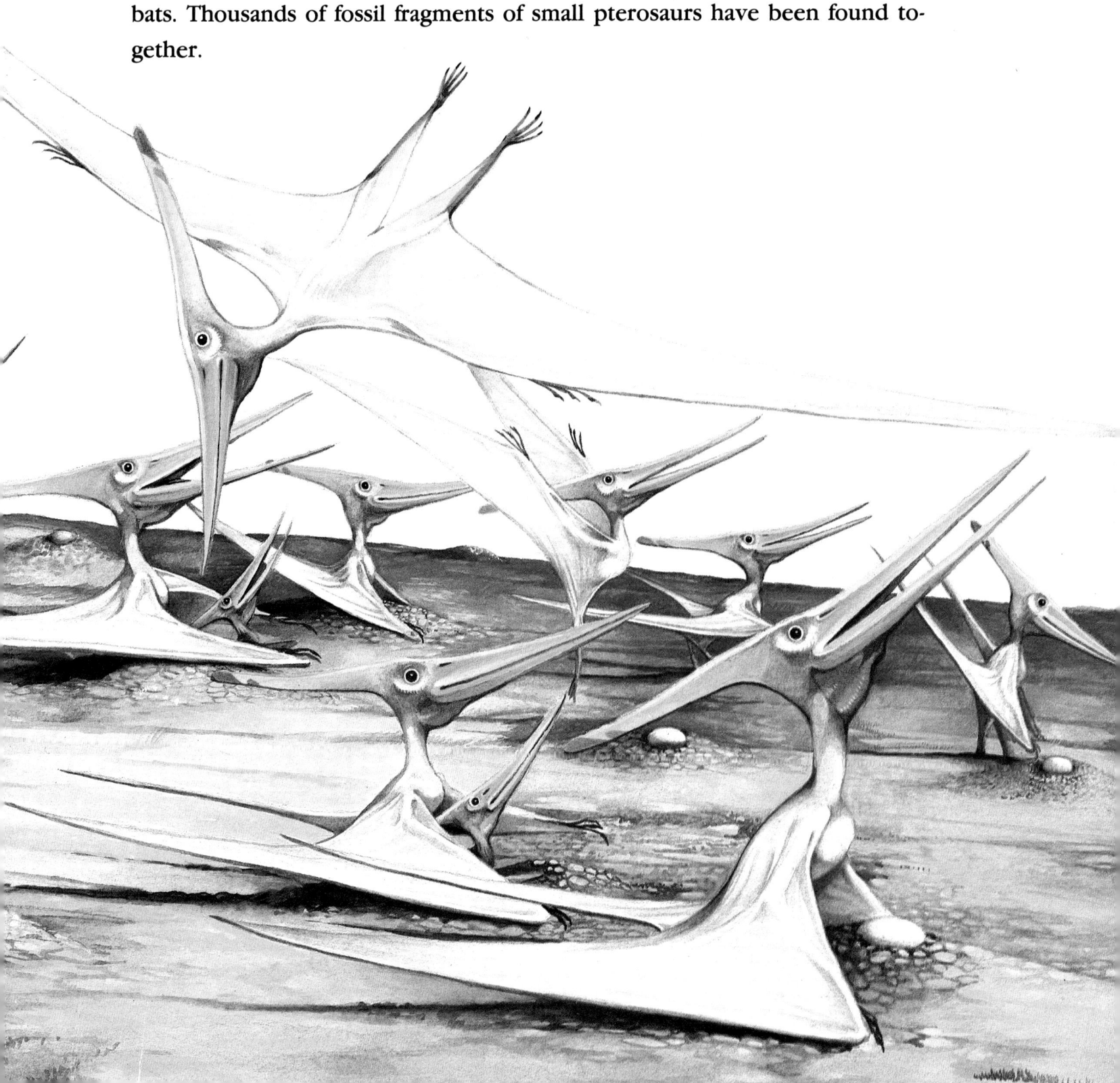

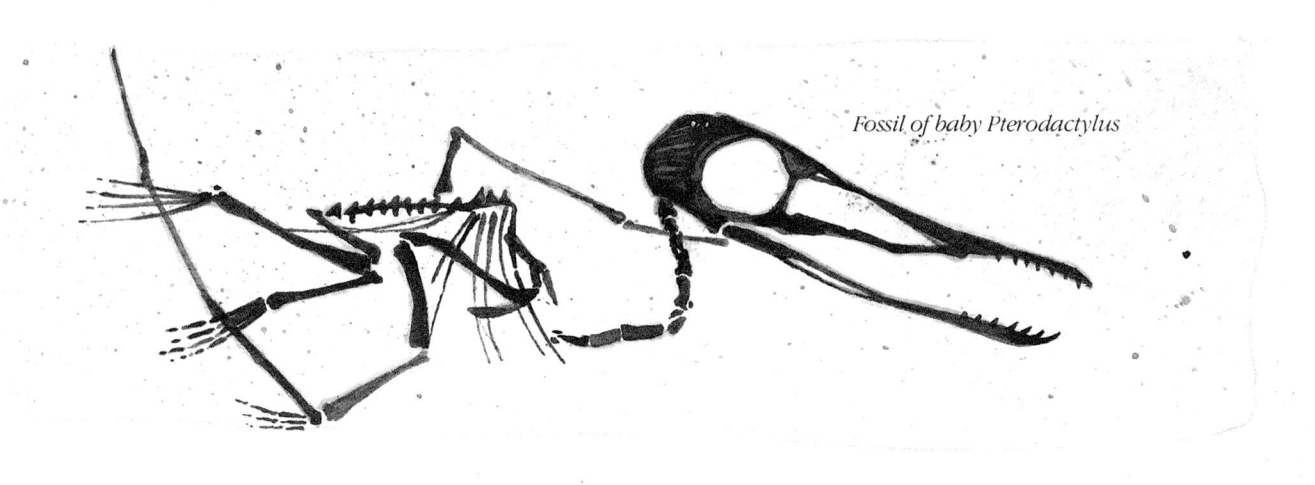

Pterosaurs have been found on every continent except Antarctica. About eighty-five species are known. Some are known from only one or two bones. Pterosaur fossils are rarely found because their skeletons were very fragile. They usually crumbled before they were covered with sand or silt. Most of the pterosaur fossils have been discovered in chalk beds in western Kansas and England or in fine-grained limestone in Germany.

Scientists divide pterosaurs into two groups, the rhamphorhynchoids and pterodactyloids. The oldest are the rhamphorhynchoids—*Sordes pilosus* was one of these. They all had fairly short jaws, broad wings, relatively short necks, and long tails with rudders at the tip. The earliest were about the size of gulls. The largest were about the size of hawks. Most rhamphorhynchoids lived during the Jurassic Period (between 190 and 135 million years ago), along with *Diplodocus* and *Allosaurus.*

Fossil of baby Pterodactylus

Sordes pilosus and Allosaurus

Dimorphodon

The earliest pterosaurs are known from fragments found in Italy. *Eudimor-phodon*, ("true two-form teeth"), and *Peteinosaurus*, ("flying lizard"), lived during the Late Triassic Period, some 200 million years ago—about the same time as the first dinosaurs. We aren't sure what they looked like, because we have so few of their bones. However, they were closely related to the Jurassic rhamphorhynchoid, *Dimorphodon*, and may have resembled that pterosaur, although they were somewhat smaller.

Dimorphodon, whose name means "two-form teeth," must have been a strange looking animal. Its total length was about forty inches. Its hawk-size body had a slender, naked tail about twenty inches long. Its neck was strong and supported an enormous eight-inch head, which was larger than its six-inch body. The jaws ended in a short beak that was lined with many sharp, pointed teeth. Those in front were large, while the teeth in back were small.

This pterosaur probably was not as agile in the air as later pterosaurs. Its wingspan was only four feet wide. But it probably could move well on land. Its legs were long and powerful.

Dimorphodon

Dimorphodon may have eaten insects, but it had a pelican-like pouch under its lower jaw. It is possible that it was a beachcomber, like shore birds of today. This pterosaur lived throughout most of the Jurassic Period. Its fossils have been found in England and central Europe.

Dimorphodon

Campylognathoides

Other rhamphorhynchoids lived in Europe about the same time as *Dimor-phodon*. *Campylognathoides*, or "curved jaw," has been found in England, Germany, and India. It was smaller than *Dimorphodon*. Its body was only three and a half inches long. Its head was much smaller in proportion to its body and the legs were shorter. But its tail was two inches longer. Its wingspan was about the same as *Dimorphodon's*, about four feet.

Campylognathoides was probably a better flyer. It may have lived near inland lakes, swooping down to prey upon small fish or large dragonflies. Its jaws were armed with teeth that curved downward and ended in a toothless beak, which was more pointed than the beak of *Dimorphodon*.

Dorygnathus, "spear-shape jaw," was closely related to *Campylongnathoides*, but was about the same size as *Dimorphodon*, about forty inches long with a forty-four-inch wingspan. Its head was even longer than *Dimorphodon's*. Long teeth stuck out at an angle from the front of its spear-shaped beak. Shorter teeth lined the back of the jaws. We know that this pterosaur was a fish-eater, because fossil fish have been found in its rib cage. It may have lived along sea and lake shores of central Europe about the same time as *Dimorphodon* did.

Scaphognathus, or "scoop jaw," was quite similar to *Dorygnathus*. But it lived later, nearer the end of the Jurassic Period. It had teeth in only the front of its very long jaws. They were straight and set far apart. This pterosaur's hawk-size body had a four-foot wingspan; large hind limbs; and a short, thick tail. Its fossils have been found in England and Germany.

Scaphognathus

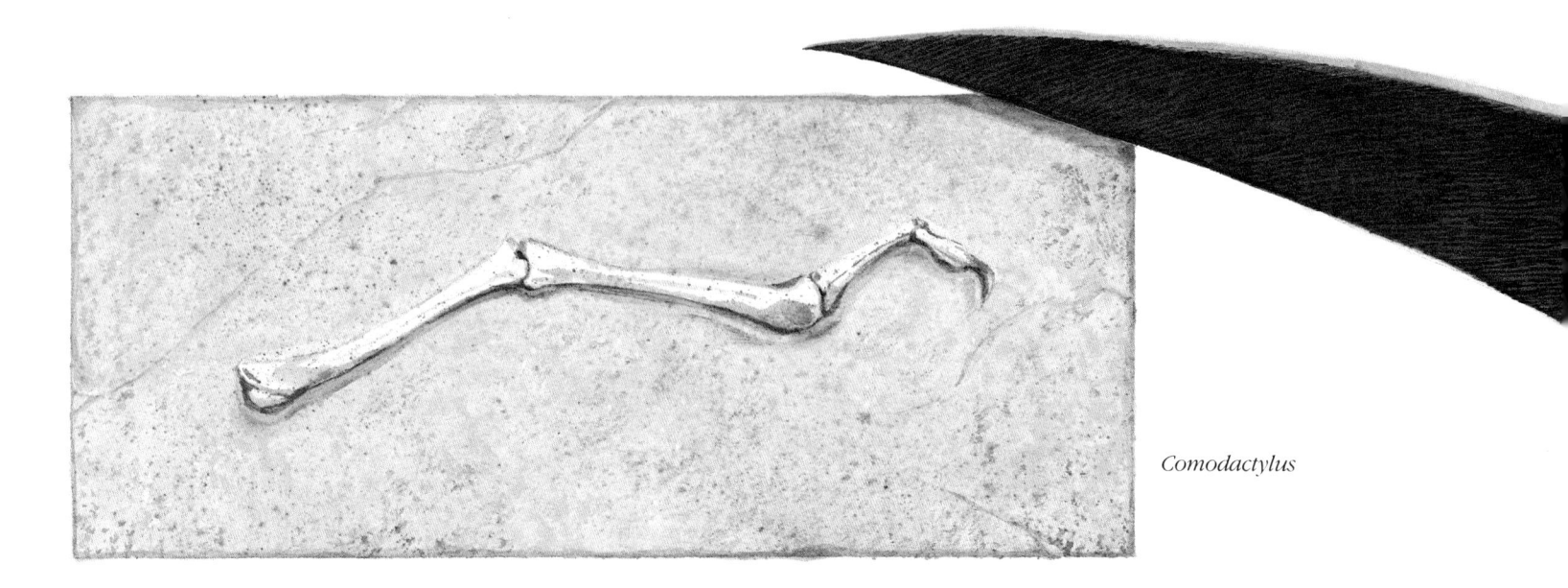

Comodactylus

Evidence of the largest rhamphorhynchoid pterosaur was recently discovered in Late Jurassic rock at Como Bluff, Wyoming. *Comodactylus* is known from a single finger bone, but it was an exciting discovery because it is the first rhamphorhynchoid found on the North American continent. Scientists think that it resembled *Dimorphodon* or *Campylognathoides,* except it was larger. *Comodactylus* means "finger bone from Como."

A partial skeleton of another rhamphorhynchoid was found in Cuba. *Nesodactylus*, "island finger," is the only other rhamphorhynchoid known from the Western Hemisphere. *Nesodactylus* probably resembled *Rhamphorhynchus*.

Rhamphorhynchus, "prow beak," was the first of the long-tailed pterosaurs discovered. It is the most common and the best known of this group. It was also one of the latest. This pterosaur had enormously long, narrow wings and was a powerful flyer—better than earlier kinds. It had a very long, stiff tail that ended in a flat, kite-shape rudder. It is the only one known to have had a rudder. Scientists think that other rhamphorhynchoids probably had rudders, but they were not preserved.

Rhamphorhynchus

The tail of **Rhamphorhynchus** was one and a half times as long as its pigeon-size body. The slender legs were short. Its eight-inch head was longer than its neck and body together. The prow-shape jaws ended in a toothless, dagger-like beak. Behind the beak there were large, widely spaced, alligator-like teeth.

Rhamphorhynchus (4-foot wingspan and pigeon-size body)

Rhamphorhynchus has been found in Germany, Portugal, and East Africa, where it probably lived, like sea gulls, along seashores. And like gulls, it probably skimmed low over the water and caught fish on the wing, swallowing them whole.

Anurognathus, "tailless jaw," was a tiny, sparrow-size pterosaur. Scientists think that it was an insect-eater. Like most rhamphorhynchoids, it had a large head with short jaws and pointed, peglike teeth. But its tail was short like the second group of pterosaurs, the pterodactyloids. This unusual rhamphorhynchoid had strong ankles and a fifth toe that extended backward. It was found in Germany, where it had been buried on the floor of a Late Jurassic lagoon.

Anurognathus

Batrachognathus

A close relative, *Batrachognathus*, "frog jaw," was found in the Soviet Union. Like *Anurognathus*, its head was large and its tail was short. Scientists think that these two tiny, Late Jurassic pterosaurs may have been linking forms between the rhamphorhynchoids and the pterodactyloids.

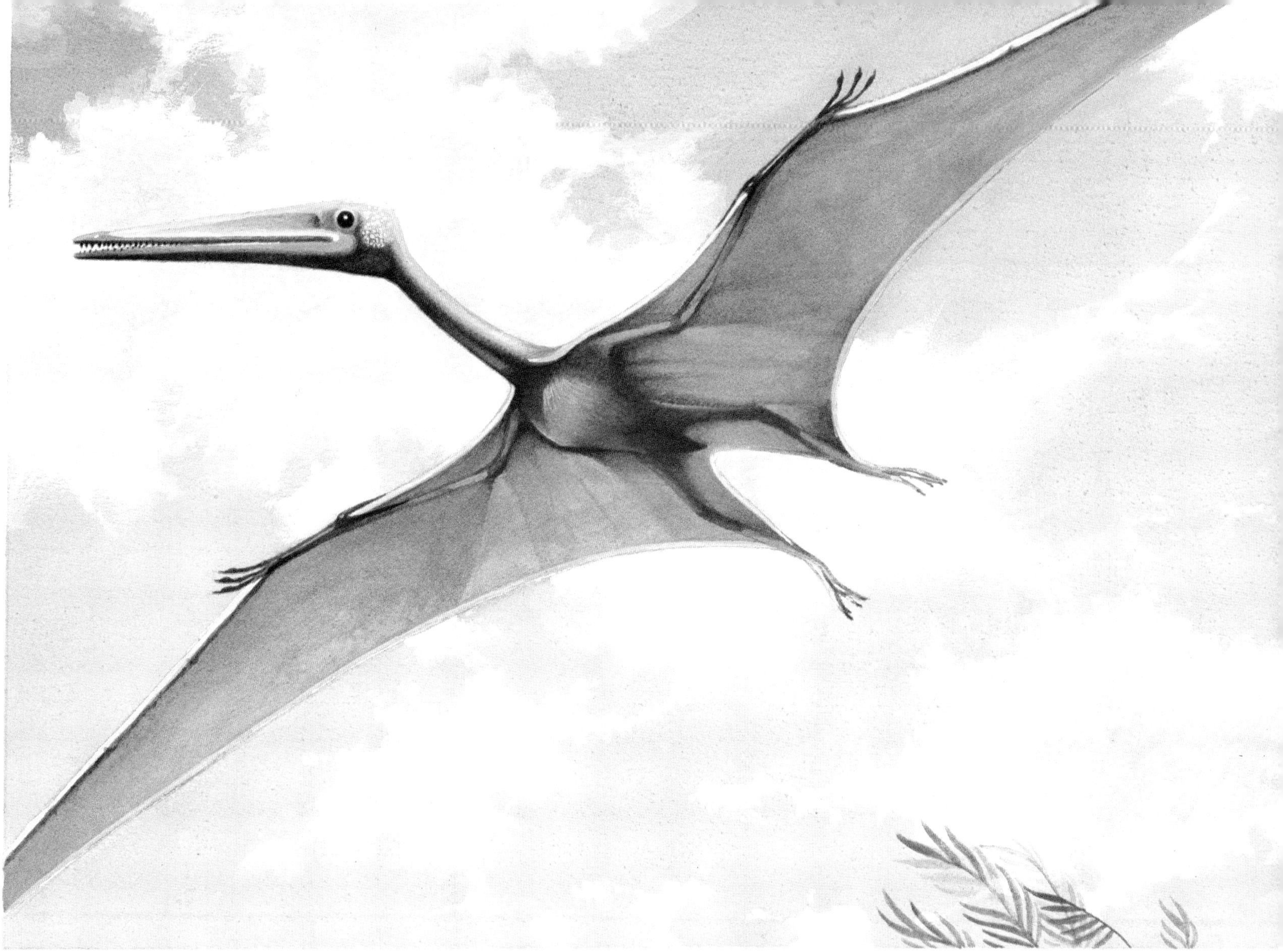

A Pterodactyloid

Pterodactyloids appeared during the Late Jurassic Period, 50 million years later than rhamphorhynchoids. The two kinds lived side by side until the rhamphorhynchoids died out at the end of the period.

Pterodactyloids were more advanced than the earlier types. They had long curved necks, long heads, long wings, and almost no tail at all. Early pterodactyloids were quite small. Most have been found in Germany. Only three are known from the Western Hemisphere. The oldest in North America, ***Dermodactylus***, "skin-finger," and ***Laopteryx,*** "fossil wing," are known from fragments found in Wyoming. A few pterosaur bones, named ***Herbstosaurus***, were found in Argentina.

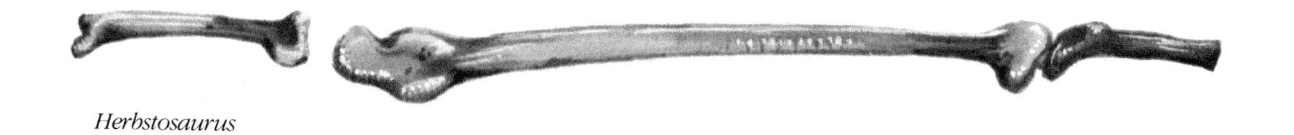

Herbstosaurus

Pterodactylus

The very first pterosaur discovered was *Pterodactylus*. Its name means "wing finger." For a long time, all pterosaurs were called pterodactyls. Now scientists call only the short-tailed pterosaurs by that name.

The body of an adult *Pterodactylus* was hawk-size with a twenty-two-inch wingspan. Its head and neck together were twice as long as its body. The long, pointed jaws had only a few teeth set in the front.

Young *Pterodactylus* were quite small. The smallest pterosaur known, first named *Ptenodracon*, "winged dragon," was the size of a small sparrow. Its head was only an inch long. It is now believed to be a juvenile *Pterodactylus*. The somewhat larger *Cycnorhamphus*, "swanlike beak," is also now believed to be a young *Pterodactylus*. Its wingspan was nineteen inches long.

Germanodactylus originally was assumed to be a species of *Pterodactylus*. It was found in the same deposits in which *Pterodactylus* was found in Germany, and was about the same size. The two looked similar, except the snout of *Germanodactylus* was shorter and more pointed and was adorned by a narrow bony crest that may have supported a hairy fringe. The teeth did not come to the tip of the snout. *Germanodactylus* may have been the ancestor of the Cretaceous *Dsungaripterus*.

Pterodactylus and *Germanodactylus* were common along the Late Jurassic and Early Cretaceous shorelines of Europe and Africa. They probably caught insects in the air.

Hatching Pterodactylus

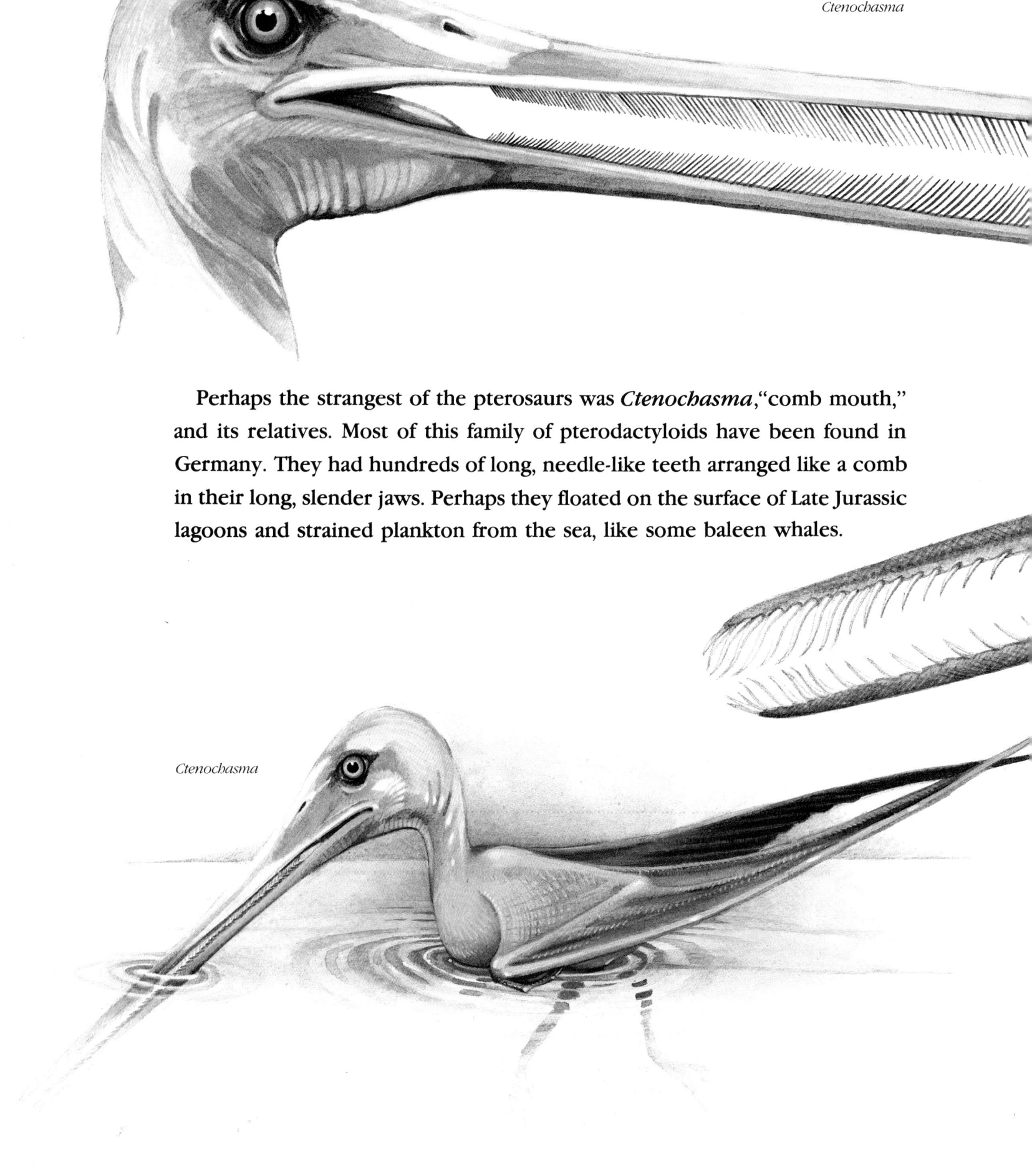

Ctenochasma

Perhaps the strangest of the pterosaurs was *Ctenochasma*, "comb mouth," and its relatives. Most of this family of pterodactyloids have been found in Germany. They had hundreds of long, needle-like teeth arranged like a comb in their long, slender jaws. Perhaps they floated on the surface of Late Jurassic lagoons and strained plankton from the sea, like some baleen whales.

Ctenochasma

Ctenochasma had 360 teeth, but its entire skull was only six inches long. *Gnathosaurus*, "jaw lizard," had similar teeth. However, this plankton-eater was one of the largest of the Jurassic short-tailed pterosaurs. Its skull was eleven inches long. A high, bony comb topped its long, slender snout.

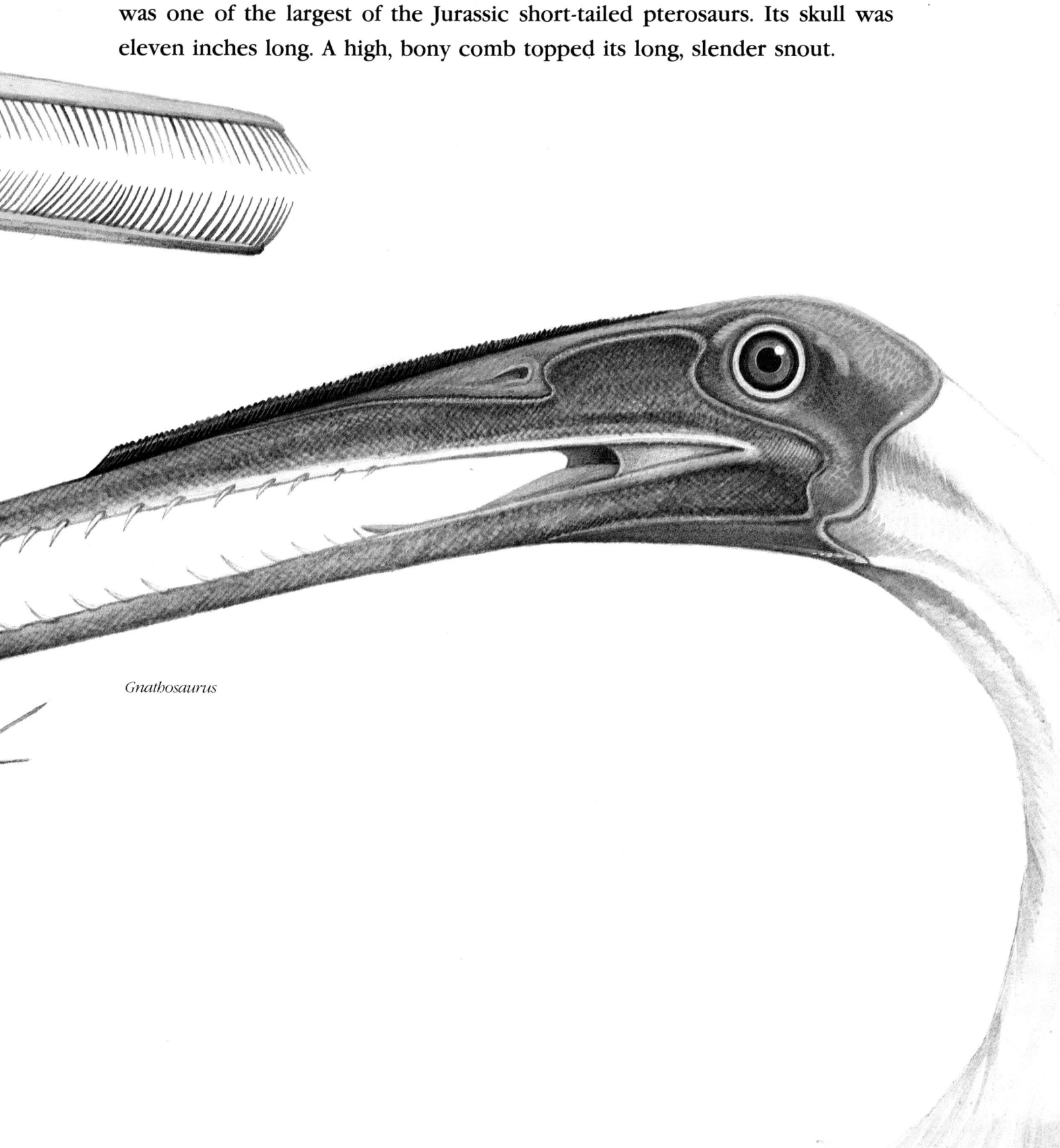

Gnathosaurus

Pterodaustro

A similar plankton-eating pterosaur lived in Early Cretaceous Argentina about 100 million years ago. *Pterodaustro*, "winged and hairy," had hundreds of very fine teeth, resembling baleen, in its lower jaw. The jaws were unusually long and curved upward. This pterosaur had a wingspan of about three and a half feet.

Other pterodactyloids lived in Early Cretaceous South America. Fragments of *Puntanipterus*, "sharp wing," were found in Argentina. A four-foot wing of *Araripesaurus*, "lizard from Araripe," was discovered in Brazil.

Dsungaripterus

Most Cretaceous pterodactyls were larger than Jurassic kinds. *Dsungarip-terus*, "Dsungaria winged lizard," had a twelve-foot wingspan. This large, dragon-like creature was found in Early Cretaceous rock in western China. Teeth lined the back part of its jaws, but the rather short, spikelike beak in front was toothless and curved upward as in some shore birds of today. The beak may have been used to spear fish.

A part of a wing finger, similar in size to that of *Dsungaripterus*, was recently discovered in Alberta. It is the first evidence of pterosaurs found in Canada.

Ornithodesmus, "bird ancestor," one of the best known of Early Creta-ceous pterosaurs of England, had a fifteen-foot wingspan and a twenty-inch head. The tip of its long snout was armed with many teeth. In spite of its name, it was not an ancestor of birds.

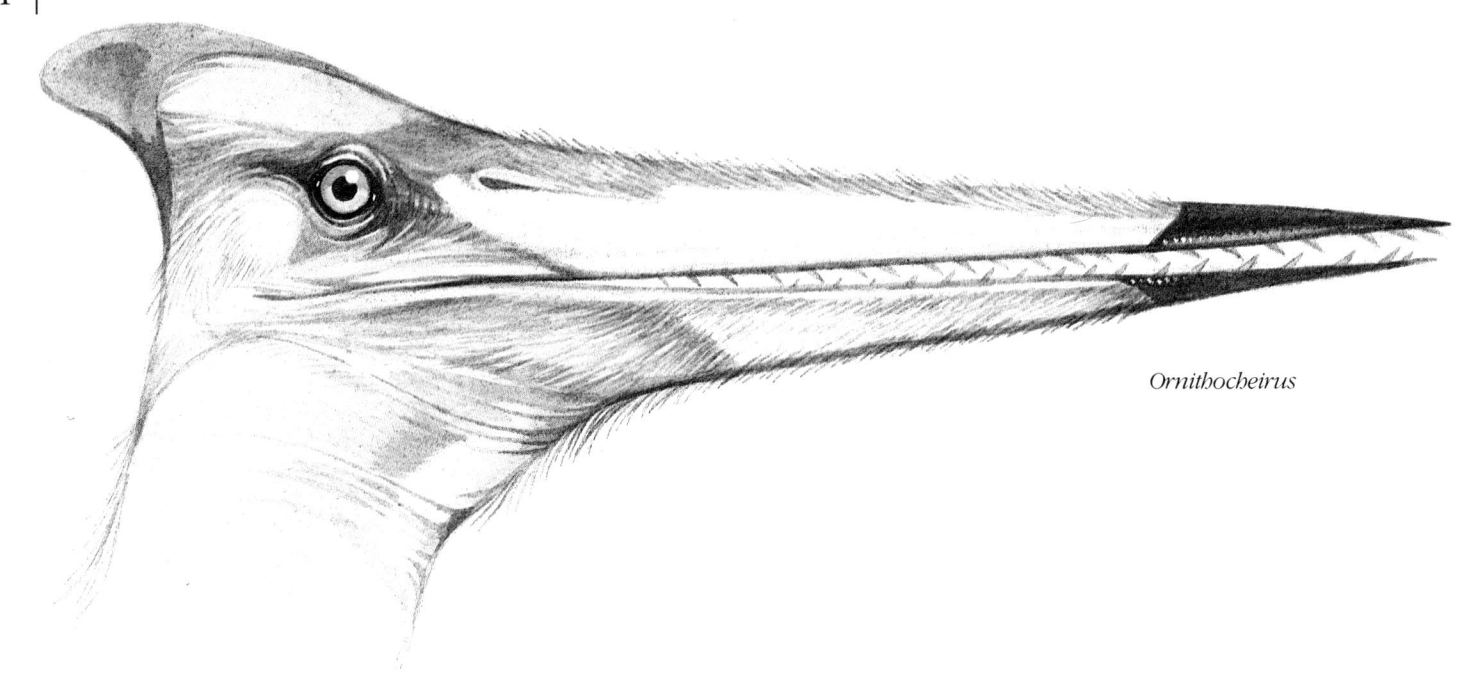

Ornithocheirus

Ornithocheirus, "bird hand," another common pterosaur in Early Creta-ceous England, was quite unlike other pterodactyls. This rather large pterosaur had a very long snout armed with many powerful, widely spaced teeth. Two long canine-like teeth projected forward from the front of its short, deep jaws. The eighteen-inch head was cone-shaped, tapering to a point like the beak of a heron. A three-inch crest projected from the rear. Its neck was massive, but birdlike. Its tail was moderately long, but much shorter than those of rhamphorhynchoids. *Ornithocheirus* also has been found in Czechoslovakia.

Another pterosaur of this period, known only from a few bones found in England, was named *Criorhynchus*, "ram beak," for its massive, unusually short, rounded skull. It had only a few large teeth.

Late Cretaceous pterosaurs were even larger than Early Cretaceous kinds. *Pteranodon*, "winged and toothless," was one of the largest, but still was extraordinarily light-weight. Its turkey-size body weighed only thirty-three pounds. Its air-filled bones were almost as thin as eggshells but were strengthened by crosswise struts, like the ribs of an airplane wing. Its long, narrow wings stretched thirty feet from tip to tip.

Pteranodon

Pteranodon was a good flyer and could have flown great distances and for long periods. Tests show that it could have glided as slowly as twelve miles per hour without falling. It was built remarkably like a modern hang glider—except that it had flexible wings. New studies suggest that it was best suited for slow flapping flight but probably could have flown up to thirty miles per hour. To get off the ground, *Pteranodon* probably needed to flap only the tips of its wings.

Pteranodon

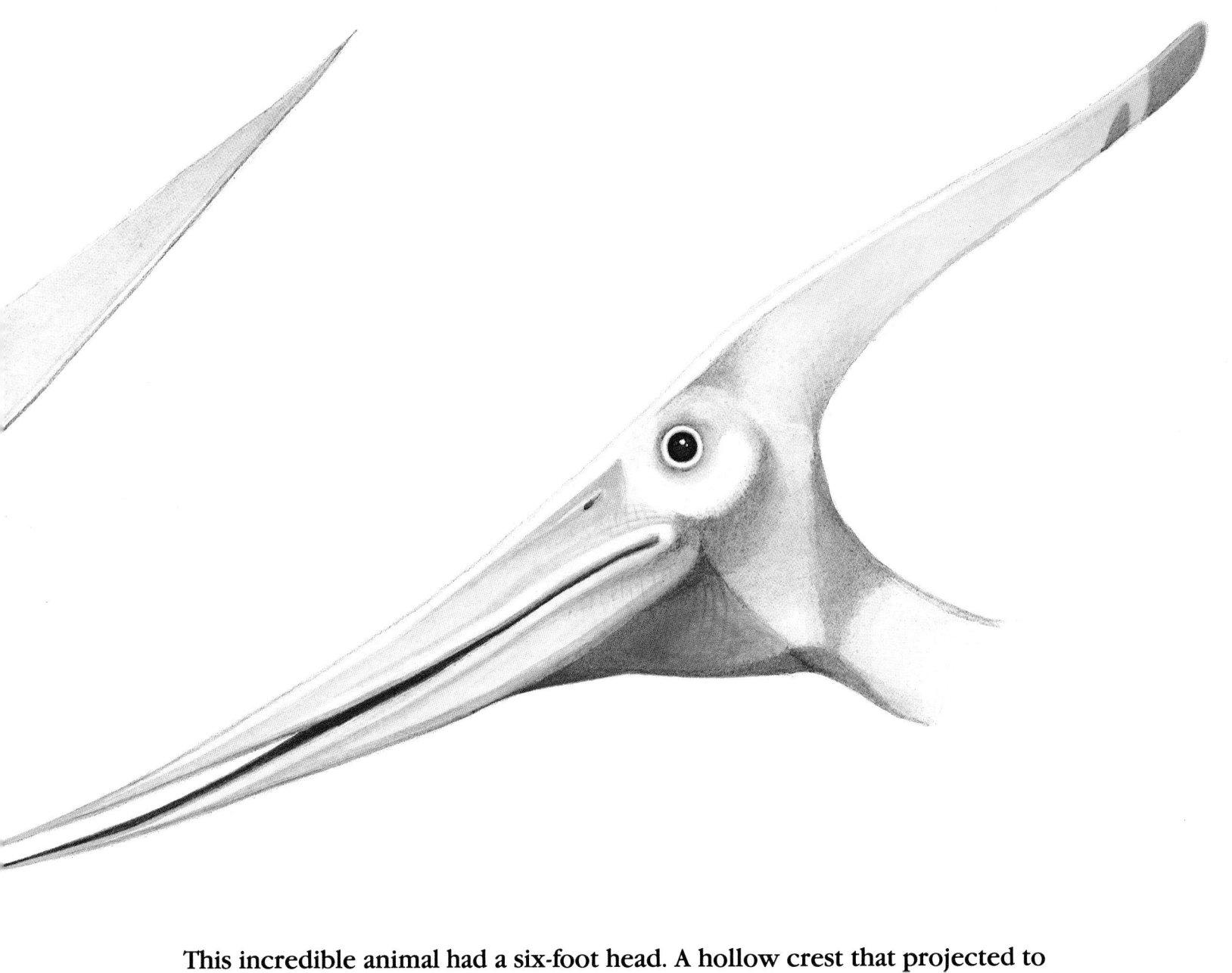

This incredible animal had a six-foot head. A hollow crest that projected to the rear balanced its long, toothless beak. The exact purpose of this crest is unknown. It may have supported a membrane that acted as an air brake used in landing or as a front-end rudder, since this pterosaur had no tail.

Pteranodon probably lived close to water and spent most of its life hunting fish, either on the wing or on the surface of the sea. It has been suggested that it was covered with white fur to camouflage it from sharks, elasmosaurs, and tylosaurs. *Pteranodon* was well equipped for spearing fish. It had a spearlike beak with a horny sheath, a pelican-like pouch, and a strong neck that was as long as its body.

Although it has been found in many parts of the world, including England and Australia, most have been found in the Niobrara chalk beds of western Kansas.

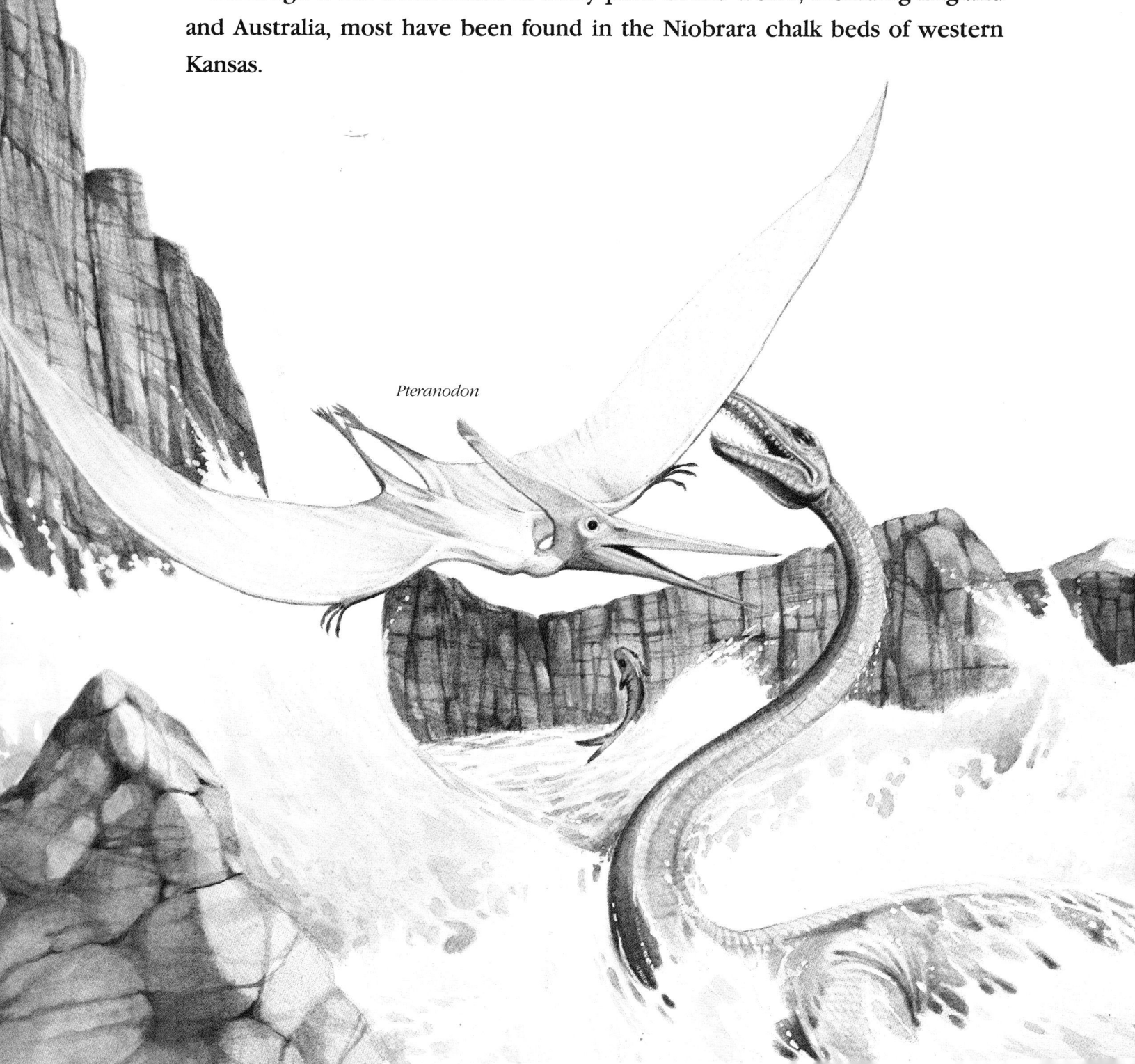

Pteranodon

Nyctosaurus

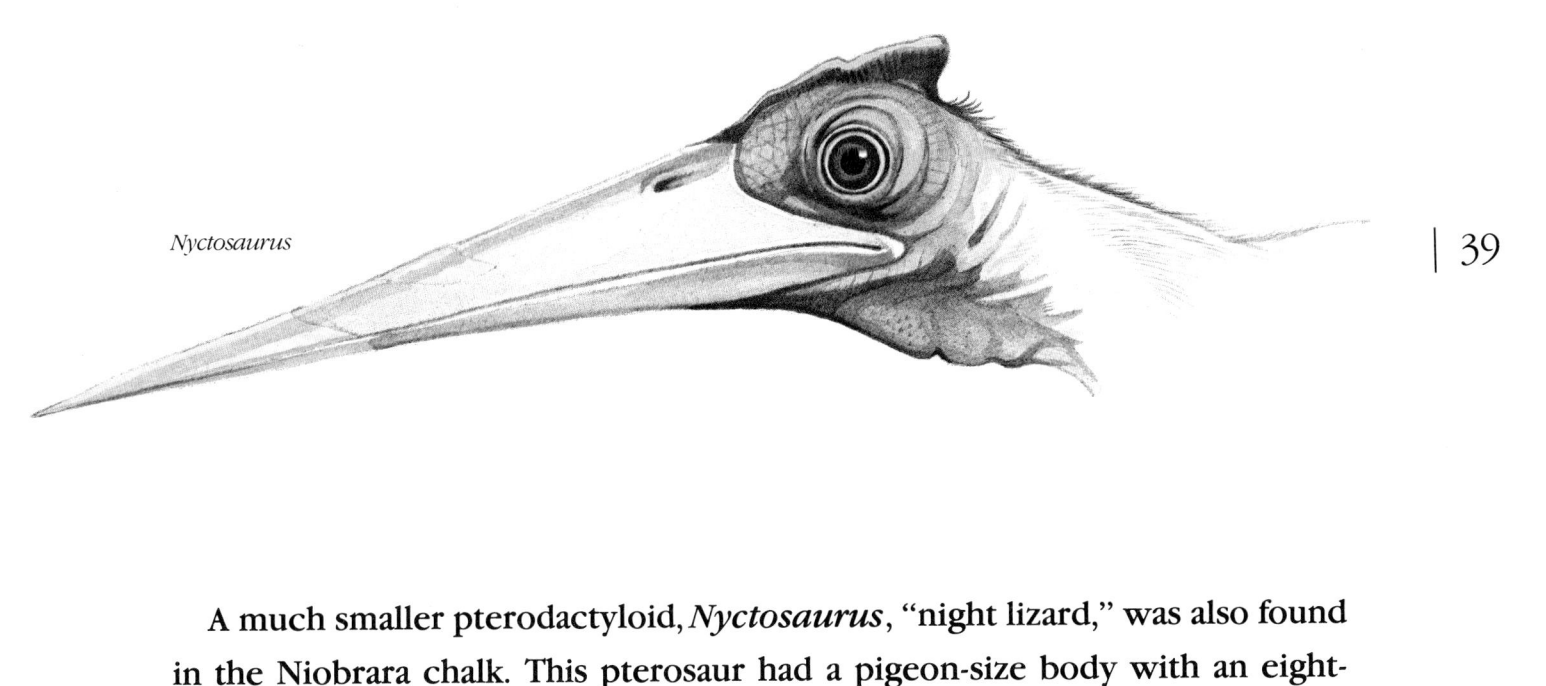

A much smaller pterodactyloid, *Nyctosaurus*, "night lizard," was also found in the Niobrara chalk. This pterosaur had a pigeon-size body with an eight-foot wingspan. Its long, narrow head had a small crest and its jaws were toothless. Some have suggested that it was a young *Pteranodon*, but others do not agree. *Nyctosaurus* has also been found in Brazil.

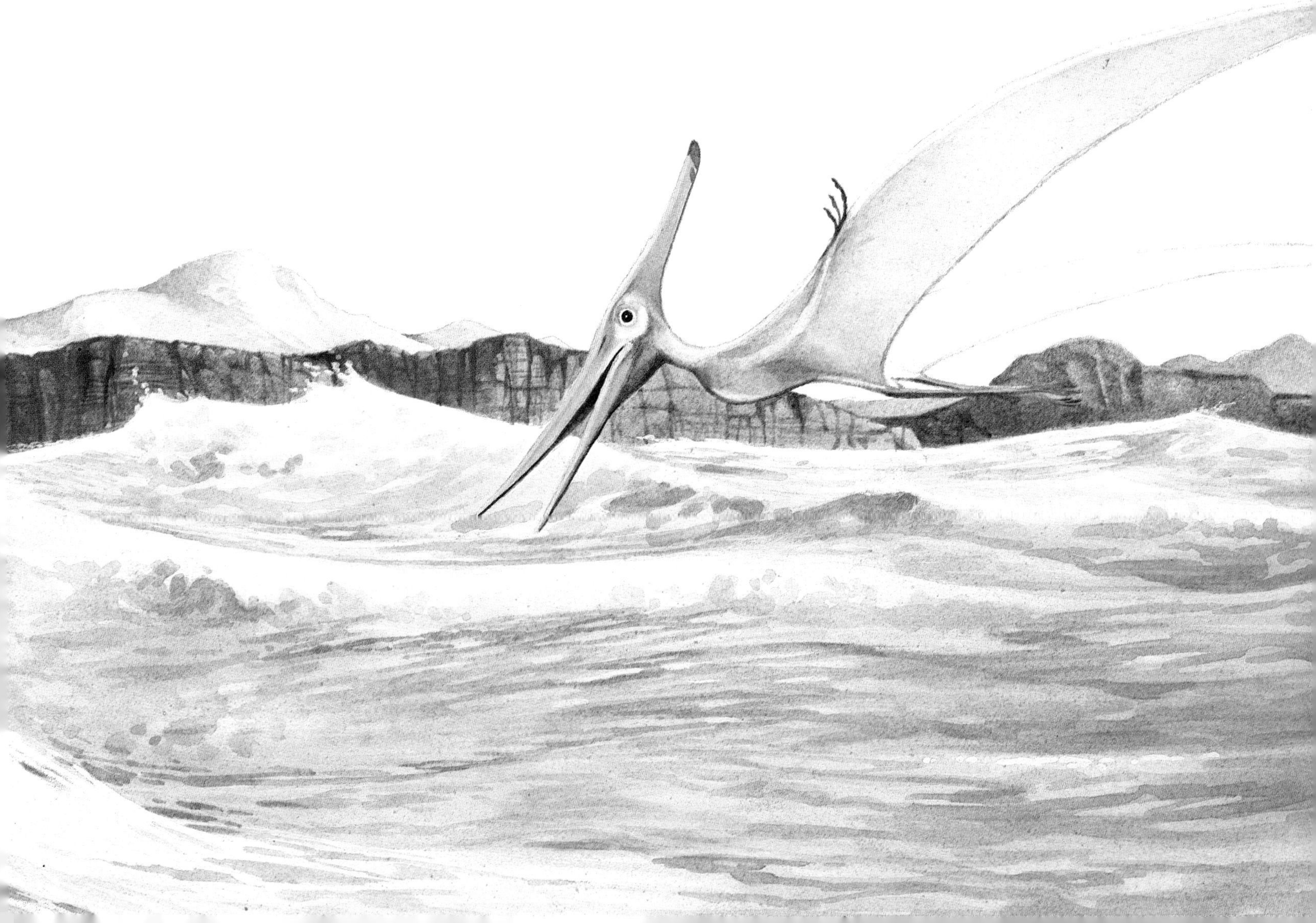

It was once thought that *Pteranodon* was the largest creature that could possibly fly. But a few years ago, a still larger pterosaur was discovered in Texas. It was named *Quetzalcoatlus* for the Aztec feathered serpent god. This 64-million-year-old pterodactyloid had a wingspan of forty to fifty feet—as big as a small airplane. It is by far the largest known flying creature. Its small head had a long, three-foot, toothless beak. The neck was very long and swanlike. The head and neck together measured eight feet in length.

Quetzalcoatlus (40-foot wingspan)

Titanosaurus

Unlike other pterosaurs, this creature may have lived on flat lowlands. It may have used its long, slender beak to probe the mud for mollusks, or it may have eaten dead animals as vultures do today. Its fossils have been found near sauropod fossils. Also like vultures, it may have used thermal updrafts to rise into the air. However, it probably needed no more than a light breeze to lift it off the ground.

Anatosaurus

This pterosaur probably ranged over most of North America. Bones believed to be those of *Quetzalcoatlus* have been found in Oregon, Wyoming, and Delaware.

Quetzalcoatlus

A similar pterosaur lived in Jordan. The neck vertebrae of a large pterosaur, which has been named *Titanopteryx*, "giant wing," were found there. They are very similar to and about the same size as those of *Quetzalcoatlus*.

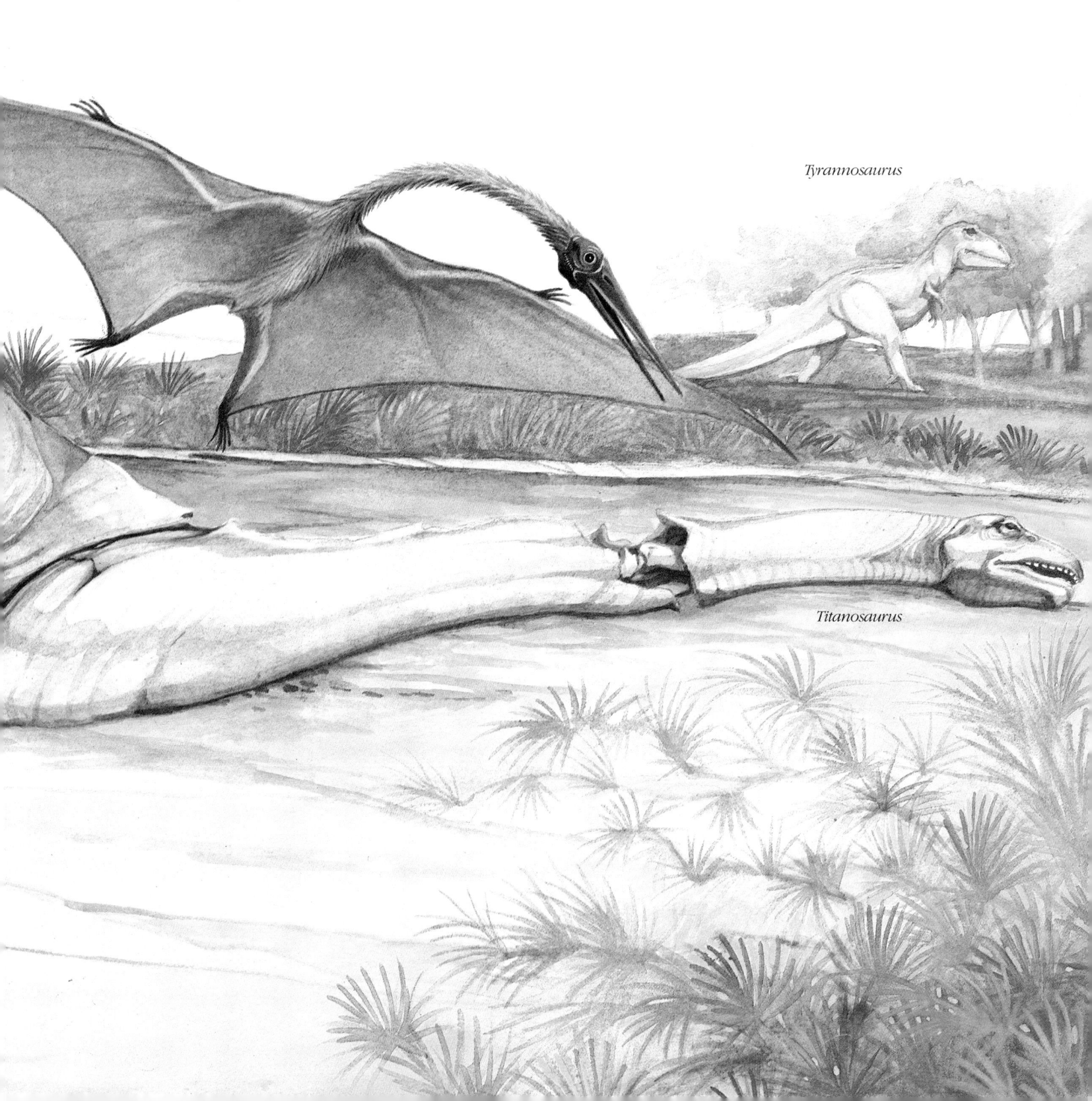

Tyrannosaurus

Titanosaurus

After the last *Quetzalcoatlus* died, there were no more pterosaurs. They all disappeared without leaving a single descendant. They became extinct near the end of the Mesozoic Era along with dinosaurs, plesiosaurs, and many kinds of plants. No one knows why, but scientists have many theories. Some suggest that too much radiation plus a cooling of the environment caused the extinction. But what caused the radiation and cooling? Perhaps it was caused by unusually heavy volcanic action, or the receding of the seas. Perhaps a supernova exploded near the earth, or maybe an asteroid collided with the earth.

Changing weather conditions may have upset the food chain, causing pterosaurs to starve to death, or they may have brought violent storms, making it impossible for enormous pterosaurs like *Pteranodon* or *Quetzalcoatlus* to fly.

Whatever caused the extinction of pterosaurs, they were magnificent creatures. These very special animals were neither birds nor mammals nor ancestors of either, yet they ruled the skies for 120 million years—a truly remarkable feat for a reptile or any animal.

PALEOZOIC ERA	MESOZOIC ERA	
PERMIAN	TRIASSIC 45 million years	JURASSIC 45 million years

THE AGE OF THE PTEROSAURS

Pterosaurs ruled the skies of the Mesozoic, from

REPTILES

RHAMPHORHYNCHOIDS

Eudimorphodon
Peteinosaurus

Campylognathoides
Dimorphodon
Dorygnathus
Nesodactylus

RHAMPHORHYNCHOIDS AND PTERODACTYLOIDS

Anurognathus R
Batrachognathus R
Comodactylus R
Ctenochasma P
Cycnorhamphus P
Dermodactylus P
Germanodactylus P
Gnathosaurus P
Herbstosaurus P
Laopteryx P
Pterodactylus P
Rhamphorhynchus R
Scaphognathus R
Sordes pilosus R

R   indicates Rhamphorhynchoid
P   indicates Pterodactyloid

THE AGE OF THE DINOSAURS

Dinosaurs evolved around the middle of the Triassic

220 million years to 65 million years ago

CENOZOIC ERA

<table>
<tr><td>CRETACEOUS
65 million years</td><td>TERTIARY
59 million years</td><td>PRESENT
QUATERNARY</td></tr>
</table>

(about 120 million years)

the late Triassic to the end of the Cretaceous.

Araripesaurus
Criorhynchus
Dsungaripterus
Ornithocheirus
Ornithodesmus
Pterodaustro
Puntanipterus

Nyctosaurus
Pteranodon
Quetzalcoatlus
Titanopteryx

PTERODACTYLOIDS

PREHISTORIC MAMMALS

MODERN MAMMALS

(about 140 million years)

and became extinct at the end of the Cretaceous.

Pronunciation Guide and Index

(Page numbers in *italic type* indicate illustrations.)